HIP-HOP

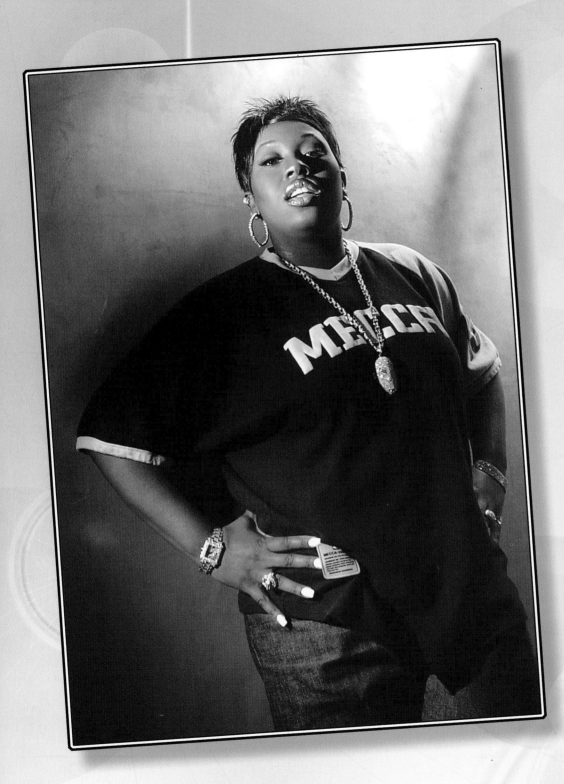

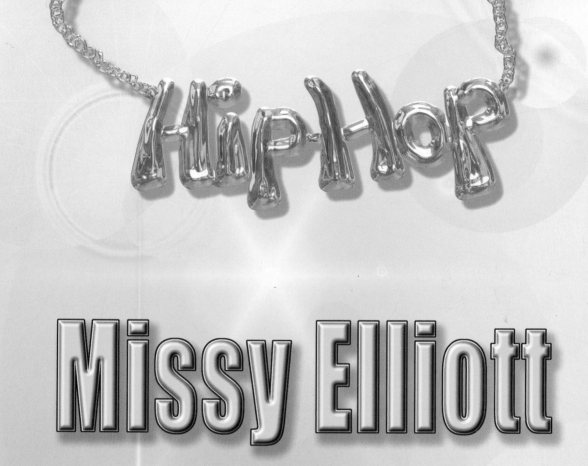

Hip-Hop

Missy Elliott

Michelle Lawlor

Mason Crest Publishers

Missy Elliott

FRONTIS Since the release of her first album, Missy Elliott has given the hip-hop
world music that challenges perceptions and makes listeners think.

PRODUCED BY 21ST CENTURY PUBLISHING AND COMMUNICATIONS, INC.

MASON CREST PUBLISHERS INC.
370 Reed Road
Broomall, Pennsylvania 19008
(866)MCP-BOOK (toll free)
www.masoncrest.com

Printed in Malaysia.

9 8 7 6 5 4 3 2

Library of Congress Cataloging-in-Publication Data

Lawlor, Michelle.
    Missy Elliott / Michelle Lawlor.
        p. cm. — (Hip-hop)
    Includes bibliographical references (p.   ) and index.
ISBN-13: 978-1-4222-0117-6
ISBN-10: 1-4222-0117-1
    1. Elliott, Missy. 2. Singers—United States—Biography—Juvenile literature.
3. Rap musicians—United States—Biography—Juvenile literature. I. Title.
II. Series.
ML3930.E45L39 2007
782.421649092—dc22
[B]   2006011804

Publisher's notes:
• All quotations in this book come from original sources, and contain the spelling
  and grammatical inconsistencies of the original text.

• The Web sites mentioned in this book were active at the time of publication.
  The publisher is not responsible for Web sites that have changed their addresses
  or discontinued operation since the date of publication. The publisher will review
  and update the Web site addresses each time the book is reprinted.

Contents

Hip-Hop Timeline

1970s Hip-hop as a cultural movement begins in the Bronx, New York City.

1974 Hip-hop pioneer Afrika Bambaataa organizes the Universal Zulu Nation.

1988 *Yo! MTV Raps* premieres on MTV.

1985 *Krush Groove*, a hip-hop film about Def Jam Recordings, is released featuring Run-D.M.C., Kurtis Blow, LL Cool J, and the Beastie Boys.

1970s DJ Kool Herc pioneers the use of breaks, isolations, and repeats using two turntables.

1979 The Sugarhill Gang's song "Rapper's Delight" is the first hip-hop single to go gold.

1986 Run-D.M.C. are the first rappers to appear on the cover of *Rolling Stone* magazine.

1970 **1980** **1988**

1976 Grandmaster Flash & the Furious Five pioneer hip-hop MCing and freestyle battles.

1986 Beastie Boys' album *Licensed to Ill* is released and becomes the best-selling rap album of the 1980s.

1970s Break dancing emerges at parties and in public places in New York City.

1982 Afrika Bambaataa embarks on the first European hip-hop tour.

1970s Graffiti artist Vic pioneers tagging on subway trains in New York City.

1988 Hip-hop music annual record sales reaches $100 million.

1984 *Graffiti Rock*, the first hip-hop television program, premieres.

1993 Rapper Snoop Dogg's album *Doggystyle* is the first debut album to hit the music charts at number one.

2006 Queen Latifah becomes the first hip-hop artist to receive a *star* on the Hollywood Walk of Fame.

1989 DJ Jazzy Jeff & The Fresh Prince become the first hip-hop artists to win a Grammy Award.

2003 Rapper Eminem becomes the first hip-hop artist to win an Academy Award.

2005 Hip-hop artist Kanye West appears on the cover of *Time* magazine.

1989 Rap is added as a new category to the *Billboard* charts.

1997 East Coast rapper Notorious B.I.G. (aka Biggie Smalls) is murdered.

2004 First National Hip-Hop Political Convention is held in Newark, New Jersey.

1989   2000   2006

1990s Hip-hop emerges in Europe.

1996 West Coast rapper Tupac Shakur is shot and killed.

2005 Rapper Will Smith opens the Philadelphia Live 8 concert as part of 10 simultaneous concerts held worldwide to bring attention to the extreme poverty in Africa.

1989 First gangsta rap album, *Straight Outta Compton*, is released by N.W.A.

2001 The hip-hop political action group, Hip-Hop Summit Action Network, is founded by Russell Simmons.

2006 The Smithsonian Institute National Museum of American History announces the creation of a new hip-hop exhibition scheduled to open in three to five years.

1992 Dr. Dre's album *The Chronic* is released; it redefines West Coast rap.

Missy Elliott's first music video was for her single "The Rain (Supa Dupa Fly)." The video was unlike any rap video MTV viewers had ever seen. Her vision of rap music was as a medium for comedy, not violence.

1

Supa Dupa Fly

When her first music video, "The Rain (Supa Dupa Fly)," aired in 1997, Missy Elliott bewildered millions of MTV viewers. Costumed in an inflated black patent-leather suit and bouncing around like a human balloon, she looked like an alien in a black garbage bag. But Missy's unconventional appearance reflected a creative musical style that would make her a superstar.

No one had ever seen a video like Missy's before. A fish-eye lens distorted her "garbage bag"-clad body, making her appear larger than life as she peered through futuristic sunglasses, rapping and dancing over a loop of Ann Peeble's song "I Can't Stand the Rain." Viewers liked what they saw. After the odd, yet compelling, video aired on prime time MTV, everyone wanted to know who this new rapper was.

Before the release of her video, Missy Elliott had been best known for writing and producing music for other artists, and occasionally vocalizing on their records. But with the success of "The Rain (Supa Dupa Fly)," the small-town southern girl who'd largely worked behind the scenes hit the big time—and fast.

Director Hype Williams worked with Missy on making the video. In an interview with *Rolling Stone*, Missy described the problems they encountered getting her suited up in the infamous costume. "It was crazy," she admitted. "You have to think about being pumped up full of air at a gas station and having to walk down the street, and you're like, at least 400 pounds." Williams hadn't thought through the process of inflating Missy, either. After he brought her to the gas station where the air pump was located and inflated her suit, she was too big to fit in the car. Missy ended up having to walk back to the set on her own.

Getting in and out of the suit itself had been an ordeal, she recalled. "It might not look that big on TV, but it really was about that big," she explained. "It took 25 minutes to get in it and 25 minutes to get out of it." Performing in the unusual outfit hadn't been easy, either. "It was very hot in there," Missy explained, "because it was extremely tight around the wrists and ankles, to keep all the air trapped inside."

However, the human balloon image is only one part of "The Rain (Supa Dupa Fly)" video. Through costume and set changes, viewers watch Missy transform her appearance again and again in creative and humorous ways. In one scene she's wearing the inflatable suit, then she's dancing in yellow overalls on a rainy street, then dressed in white on a computer-imaged hillside, then driving off in her Hummer. The video mixes quick shots of various scenes with blink-and-you'll-miss-them computer generated special effects.

When Missy's first video first aired, its creative vision and individual style of music got the young rapper noticed. However, it was the entire album *Supa Dupa Fly* that established her place in the world of hip-hop. Missy had a sound that was all her own. Critics had a tough time placing her into just one category because her music blended so many **genres**—hip-hop, rap, R&B, and even a little pop. What the album made clear was that Missy was an innovator: a female rapper, a rhythm and blues (R&B) singer, writer, and producer.

And Missy wasn't afraid to do her own thing. Her humorous, lighthearted style of rapping was entertaining, while her R&B vocals sprinkled throughout the record gave listeners a hint of the emotional woman inside. She was a complex person—honest, funny, emotionally mature, and good at finding a catchy hook.

This photo shows the cover of Missy Elliott's first single, "The Rain (Supa Dupa Fly)," from the album *Supa Dupa Fly*. The song made her an MTV icon, and the platinum-selling album made her a hip-hop star.

Her phrasing ability and off-the-cuff rapping style brought her lots of attention and critical acclaim.

In the early 1990s, while other rappers were talking about violence and murder, Missy was asking "Who's got the keys to the Jeep?" and chuckling in the background. Delivering off-kilter rhymes with her laid-back southern drawl, she had a friendly, girl-around-the-corner appeal. The guest appearances on her album were tastefully done and

THE SOURCE

THE MAGAZINE OF HIP-HOP MUSIC, CULTURE & POLITICS

MISSY &
TIMBALAND
BEATS & RHYMES
FROM THE MATRIX

NOREAGA
LESS RUNNIN'/MO EATIN'

SLICK RICK
ORIGINAL DON DADA

EXCLUSIVE!
WILL PUFF DADDY
DO TIME?

'99 SUMMER
GUIDE:
MUSIC,
MOVIES
AND MORE

PLUS:
LIL' CEASE
HIP-HOP BODYGUARDS

JULY 1999 · NO.118
US $2.95 · UK £2.50 · CANADA $3.50

This 1999 cover of *The Source* magazine features Missy Elliott and her longtime production partner Timbaland. Thanks to their fresh ideas of what hip-hop music could be, Missy and Timbaland had an opportunity to write and produce music for many famous rappers.

gave listeners a sense of her versatility with the wide range of artists with whom she **collaborated**.

Missy owed some of her innovative sound to the contributions of her good friend Tim Mosely, better known as Timbaland, who had an uncanny ability to create dynamic beats using unusual arrangements, sounds, and instrumentation. **Sampling** beats from various musical styles, Missy and Timbaland had set the standard for the sound of hip-hop in the late 1990s. They not only sampled other artists' works, but created their own tracks as well.

With the release of *Supa Dupa Fly*, Missy secured her spot in history as one of the first female hip-hop icons. In October 1997 *Spin* magazine praised the first album:

> **"*Supa Dupa Fly* is distinctive, cohesive, and innovative enough to wind up as the most influential pop record since Dr. Dre's *The Chronic*. Elliott's proficiency with a hook is unerring; everything here has 'hit' stamped all over it."**

"The Rain (Supa Dupa Fly)" video put a face to the name Missy Elliott. However, the girl in the garbage bag was just getting started. The world would be hearing much more from Missy in the years to come, as her exceptional writing, producing, and vocal abilities would propel her to the top.

Missy Elliott poses on the stoop of a house in an urban area. She spent her childhood growing up in poverty, using her music to escape from the abuse and violence that were normal at home.

2

Growing Up Missy

Singing comes naturally to Missy Elliott, who started performing when quite young. "I'd stand on the side of the road when I was just a little girl singing on [trash] cans," she explains. "People would roll down their windows and laugh, saying 'isn't she cute.'" In Missy's imaginative mind, the grimy trashcans were a huge, glittering stage.

In reality the little girl's surroundings were the gritty, low-income Portsmouth, Virginia, neighborhood in which she lived. Born in Portsmouth on July 1, 1971, Melissa "Missy" Arnette Elliott was the only child of Ronnie Elliott, a former marine, and Patricia Elliott, a dispatcher for a power company. Missy grew up in poverty, living in a home infested with rats, mice, and cockroaches.

Creative and likeable, young Missy often kept her classmates and friends laughing in school. However, despite a high IQ test score that ranked her as a genius, she did poorly in her classes. Believing the high IQ score was a fluke, Missy's teachers had her retake the test. But she repeated the high score, leaving them scratching their heads over how such a bright child could bring home F's on her report cards.

The teachers had no way of knowing that Missy was suffering through serious problems at home. When Missy was just eight years old, she had been sexually assaulted by a 16-year-old male cousin. The abuse continued for a year and stopped only after another relative found out. As a result of this trauma, Missy suffered from shame and frequent bouts of depression.

Missy was also troubled by the ongoing violence in her family. She regularly witnessed her father physically abusing her mother, sometimes causing severe injuries. Once, her father rammed Patricia Elliott's head into a wall so hard that he broke through it. Another time he pulled her arm so hard that it came out of its socket.

Although Missy's father never hit her, the young girl was afraid her father might kill her mother if no one was around to stop him. "I never wanted to go places," Missy explained in a 1999 interview with Yahoo! Music, "because I was scared my father would be beating up my mother."

Finding a Way to Deal

With so much conflict in her life, Missy would retreat to her room and find **solace** the only way she knew how: through music. "When I was little I used to sit in a room, lock the door, take my mother's broomsticks, line up my dolls and sing," Missy told *Essence* magazine in March 2000. "In my mind I pictured them screaming for me. I would go into a whole other zone."

As she performed for her imaginary fans, Missy could let go of stress and feel good. Her music comforted her during the tough times, enabling her to temporarily escape her frightening home life. During this time she developed a passion for writing and performing that she would never lose.

Missy wrote songs in the form of poems, and sang about things in her daily life. She told *Essence* magazine, "I used to write stupid little songs. Of course, they weren't stupid to me, but I used to write about butterflies and birds and stuff. I'd be out there singing hard about the roaches or whatever." Missy often wrote her song lyrics on the wallpaper of her bedroom.

As Missy grew older, her father's abusive ways continued. Finally, in 1984 Missy's mother had had enough. Patricia left Ronnie and took 13-year-old Missy with her.

As a way to forget about her troubles, Missy Elliott would hide in her room and imagine her toys as an audience, applauding her on-stage performance. She wrote her own songs about anything and everything that she found interesting, from butterflies to roaches.

Missy's Inspiration

To pay the bills as a single mom, Patricia Elliot had to work extra hours at her job with the utility company, which meant Missy was often left on her own. She filled the time writing and listening to music, gaining experiences that would later help her in her music career.

In the early 1980s the radio airwaves were dominated by what is now called **old school hip-hop**, which featured artists like Big Daddy Kane, Rakim, MC Lyte, Public Enemy, Slick Rick, and Whodini. Although Missy loved the varieties of music styles she heard, she wondered if she could find a place in the male-dominated hip-hop world.

For the most part, the women in hip-hop videos that Missy saw on MTV were rail-thin, sexy-looking models with good looks but little talent. When their looks faded, so did their careers. As a heavyset teenager standing a little over five feet tall, Missy knew she didn't fit the typical image of female hip-hop performers. But she knew she had musical talent, and she wanted to be recognized for it.

In the late 1980s Missy found the role model she needed when the first all-female hip-hop group, Salt-N-Pepa, hit it big. With their catchy songs and unique style, Salt-N-Pepa became one of the first rap groups to cross over from hip-hop to mainstream music. The group's members weren't just pretty faces. They had real talent. Missy thought that if the women in Salt-N-Pepa could find success by being themselves, so could she.

Another inspiration for Missy was her mother. As an adult Missy has told interviewers how much she admires her mother for having the courage to get herself and her only daughter out of an abusive situation. Patricia Elliott struggled to make a good life for her daughter, and that struggle made her a strong woman—someone her daughter wanted to emulate.

While in high school, Missy continued to write songs and dream big. She also penned daily fan letters to Michael and Janet Jackson, explaining her situation and desire for stardom. In her daydreams, the Jacksons would come find her, discover her talent, and help make her a star. Then Missy could give her mother the life she deserved. But Michael and Janet never responded.

A Plan of Action

In 1991, a year after graduating from high school, Missy and three neighborhood girls—LaShawn Shellman, Chonita Coleman, and

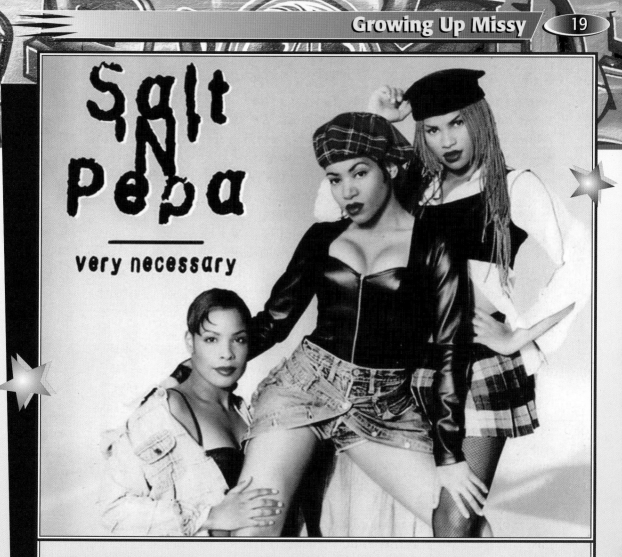

The cover of Salt-N-Pepa's 1993 album *Very Necessary*. Salt-N-Pepa was an influential group that encouraged young women to use their minds instead of just being sex objects. They became role models for a generation of female rappers, including Missy Elliott.

Radiah Scott—formed an R&B group named Fay-Z. Missy wrote almost all of the group's songs, and she booked shows for the group at local clubs and talent shows.

Fay-Z began working with DJ Tim "Timmy Tim" Mosely, who was also from Portsmouth, after Missy's friend Melvin "Magoo" Barcliff introduced them. Mosely was a talented and inventive musician who created hip-hop backing tracks on his small Casio keyboard. Missy liked his innovative style. "He happened to play some stuff," Missy later recalled. "He was just playing songs and it was still rap tracks, but I could sing over them and I started writing songs. From that point on, we just kept working together."

Missy Elliott and her friend and producer Timbaland arrive at the MAC Viva Glam V Launch dinner in London. The two have been working together since they met in Portsmouth in 1991, when Missy was part of a group called Fay-Z.

Shortly after they began working with Tim, the members of Fay-Z decided to make a move for the big time, and made a plan to get discovered. Missy learned that Jodeci, a successful **contemporary** R&B group on the Elektra Entertainment Group label, was coming to town. She and the other girls decided that if they could get DeVante Swing— Jodeci's producer, songwriter, and Elektra label talent scout—to hear Fay-Z's sound, a deal with Elektra would be sure to follow.

Missy and her hopeful group prepared for an **audition** using the music by her new friend Tim. "I made sure we had all original music," Missy remembers. "Timbaland did it for us. . . . he was doing amazing things. He only had this little Casio."

The girls bought tickets to the Jodeci concert, and Missy managed to get a backstage pass. At the concert, she found DeVante and convinced him to let the group audition after the show. Later that night, dolled up and in matching outfits, the girls made their way to DeVante's hotel room, where, as promised, they were given an audition.

DeVante Swing liked Fay-Z's sound so much that he signed them right away to Swing Mob, a subdivision label of Elektra that he headed. The four members of Fay-Z, now renamed Sista, soon found themselves on an airplane heading toward New York City.

Rapper Missy Elliott came to New York City hoping to cut her first album. When that plan fell apart, though, she was unwilling to give up. Her talent had become well known, and she refused to compromise on her music just to get a contract.

3

A Blessing in Disguise

Once in New York City, Sista began recording music for the all-important first album. At the same time an inspired Missy was also writing, using the new experiences in her life as inspiration for songs. Her creative ability impressed DeVante, who soon had her composing music for Jodeci and for other artists on the Elektra and Swing Mob labels.

As Missy worked with other artists on their records, she quickly gained perspective on what makes a successful release. The key to Sista's future success, she believed, lay in more than good vocals and clever lyrics. Good music required the right beats. Missy knew that her friend Tim Mosely had to be involved in making the group's record.

At the first opportunity, Missy told Devante that she wanted Tim to do the Sista album, describing him as "this new cat who got a sound I never heard before." After hearing some of Tim's work, DeVante agreed with Missy. He hired Tim, now christened Timbaland, who moved to New York to become part of the Swing Mob family.

By 1994 everything seemed to be falling into place. The Sista record was going well, with Timbaland creating the beats and DeVante serving as executive producer. However, as the album neared completion, record company executives decided not to release it. A music critic once described the shelved album as "one of the greatest hip hop records never released," and to this day, it remains unheard.

A year later the Swing Mob label folded, and many of its artists went their separate ways. Missy was disappointed, but not discouraged. "Being rejected can be a negative thing, but if you believe in yourself, then it's an automatic drive," she told *Interview* magazine in September 2005. "It's like 'You shut the door in my face and now look!'"

Missy wasn't about to give up her dreams of being a musician. She and Tim packed their belongings and moved back to Portsmouth, Virginia, where they set up a studio and continued to make music. The failure of Sista would prove to be a blessing in disguise, as new doors soon opened up for Missy.

Back North

DeVante had been too impressed by Missy's writing ability and Tim's fresh music style to leave them in Virginia. He convinced them to return to the New York City area and join his songwriting team. While working with DeVante's artists, Missy became good friends with fellow R&B artist and writer Faith Evans.

Faith eventually became a "test audience" for many of the new songs that Missy was writing. Missy recalled her friend's positive attitude and encouragement: "I used to be embarrassed and I used to always hold my head down when I played [my songs for her] because I didn't think they were hot." Missy explained. "And she used to be like, 'Why you always hang your head down? Your [stuff] is hot!'" Faith's friendly encouragement helped Missy gain more confidence in her writing.

Missy and Tim soon became a sought-after production team. From 1995 to 1997, they created hit singles for several artists, most notably the female R&B groups SWV ("Can We") and 702 ("Steelo"). In 1996 Missy and Timbaland began working with a 16-year-old singing sensation named Aaliyah, who was in the process of making her second album. Her husband, 28-year-old R&B singer/songwriter R. Kelly, had produced her first record. But after news of Aaliyah's real age surfaced (she had lied on her marriage license), the marriage had been annulled. R. Kelly had exited Aaliyah's life, and she had found herself without a producer.

When Timbaland was approached to take R. Kelly's place, he accepted and immediately brought Missy in on the project. As Missy, Tim, and Aaliyah worked together, they became close friends. Missy and Tim eventually wrote and produced nine tracks for *One in a Million*. After its release in August 1996, it went **double platinum**, selling more than 2 million copies.

Missy worked with R&B star Aaliyah on her second album, *One in a Million* (1996). The record was a huge success, and helped Missy's own career take off as well. Tragically, Aaliyah's life was cut short when she died in a plane crash in 2001.

Missy's writing and guest vocals, as well as Tim's skilled production, on *One in a Million* gained the duo national attention. In the music business, word travels fast about a hot new talent, especially when those contributions are on an album that goes double platinum. One deejay thought it illegal that one person could have so much musical talent, so he gave Missy the nickname **Misdemeanor**.

Fans clamored for more from Misdemeanor, the clever writer-producer who'd created so many hits for other artists. Many of Missy's admirers wanted her to make her own solo record. Missy began to consider the idea. But she knew that if she were going to make a record of her own, it had to be *really* good. And she wanted to create something totally new. "I was not going to make a record just to make one, if you know what I mean," she said.

After Sean "Puffy" Combs, a young producer at Bad Boy Records, heard Missy's contributions to Aaliyah's album, he asked her to do a guest spot on his new **remix** of Gina Thompson's single "The Things You Do." Missy agreed, and added her own signature rap to the song by topping it off by a goofy "hee-haw" giggle. This simple laugh made the song—and Missy—incredibly popular, although many listeners did not know her by name. In an interview with VH1, Missy recalled how she became famous because of her laugh in the song: "That one caused people to start coming up to me on the street and say, 'Ain't you the 'Hee Ha' girl?'"

Impressed by Missy's talent, Puffy asked her to do another spot on MC Lyte's "Cold Rock a Party." He also tried to secure an exclusive deal by signing her to Bad Boy Records, but Missy was fielding several offers. "As much as I love Puffy and I know he makes stars, I didn't want to be under him," she told *VIBE* Magazine. "I wanted to be at the same table as him drinking the same champagne. I wanted to buy *him* drinks."

Misdemeanor Makes a Deal

Before she was ready to sign any contract, Missy had several conditions. She didn't want a contract that would prevent her from continuing to write songs for herself and other artists, or from producing and performing their songs. She wanted complete control over everything that had her name on it. "I am a businesswoman *first*," Missy has said, and she means it.

Independent, self sufficient, and determined to manage herself, Missy Elliott wasn't interested in having anyone tell her what to do

Sean "P. Diddy" Combs arrives at a fashion show in New York, 2005. Combs is a talented producer who owns the record label Bad Boy Entertainment. He was impressed by Missy's talent and invited her to contribute to several of his label's releases.

when it came to make her own record. And once she finally decided to do one, a major label bidding war ensued. Choosing a record label can be difficult, as artists struggle to decide which label suits them best. However the CEO of Elektra Entertainment Group, Sylvia Rhone, made Missy's choice easy. Rhone offered Missy a recording contract *and* her own label. This kind of offer had never been made before to any artist, let alone someone essentially new to the industry.

Missy signed without hesitation, even though Elektra was the same label that had dropped her Sista album a few years earlier. Under the agreement, made in 1997, Missy got exactly what she wanted. She could continue to discover, develop, and produce for new artists. And she would have *complete* creative control over her recordings and her own label, which she named The Gold Mind, Inc. Missy became her label's first client.

Plenty of artists have owned their own record labels, but not many of them are female, and even fewer are African-American females. Like the members of Salt-N-Pepa, Missy believed she could pave the way for more female artists and producers in the music business. "I feel like I'm going to open up a lot of doors," Missy told *Rolling Stone.* "A lot of men, like Puffy, throw showcases for their artists, but females need to get out there and do stuff like this. We're just too used to this being a male-dominated field."

Supa Dupa Fly

In July 1997 Missy released her first full-length solo album, entitled *Supa Dupa Fly.* Co-produced by Timbaland, the album featured several artists and groups with whom Missy had worked in the past, including Aaliyah, 702, Busta Rhymes, Lil' Kim, and Da Brat. *Supa Dupa Fly* debuted at number three on the Billboard charts, the music industry's list of top-selling songs. The ranking was one of the highest debuts ever for a female hip-hop star. The album went on to sell more than one million copies, achieving **platinum** status.

Steve Huey of *All Music Guide* touted Missy's debut *Supa Dupa Fly* as "Arguably the most influential album ever released by a female hip-hop artist. . . . A boundary-shattering postmodern masterpiece." The masterpiece had actually been recorded in just a two-week period, with all of the writing done on the spot in the studio. While some artists spend weeks, months, even years preparing songs, Missy could write a song in about 20 minutes. "It's a God-given talent, I guess," Missy says. "I just hear the track and then feel something and then write it."

The unique video for the album's first single, "The Rain (Supa Dupa Fly)," received rave reviews. That year it was nominated for three MTV awards: Best Rap Video, Breakthrough Video, and Best Direction. It also won two *Billboard* Video Music Awards, for Best Clip (Rap) and Best New Artist Clip (Rap).

In 1998 Missy received even more recognition. She was nominated for three **Grammy** Awards: Best Rap Solo Performance, for "The Rain (Supa Dupa Fly)"; Best Rap Performance by a Duo or Group, for "Not Tonight" (with Lil' Kim, Da Brat, Lisa "Left Eye" Lopes, and Angie Martinez); and Best Rap Album, for *Supa Dupa Fly*.

Supa Dupa Fly produced several other hit singles. They included "Beep Me 911," which featured 702, Timbaland, and Magoo; "Hit 'Em with Da Hee," featuring Rapper Mocha and Timbaland; "Izzy Izzy

This image is the cover of Missy Elliott's groundbreaking first album *Supa Dupa Fly*. The cover does not attempt to market the music through sex, but rather demands that the music sell itself. And it did, to the tune of 1 million copies.

Ahh," featuring Busta Rhymes; and "Sock It 2 Me," with guest spots by Da Brat and Lil Kim. The songs on *Supa Dupa Fly* were unlike anything heard before, somewhat like conversations with Missy—good-natured, fun, and goofy at times. She was on a whole new level of hip-hop.

An Unconventional Talent

While Missy was building her label's reputation with her solo career, she was also signing other artists on her label. One talent find was R&B singer Nicole Wray. Under Missy's direction, Nicole's record *Make It Hot* went gold, selling more than 500,000 copies in 1998.

Grammy Award winner Whitney Houston poses with Missy Elliott at a press conference in New York City, 1998. Missy collaborated with Houston on her album *My Love Is Your Love* and sang on the track "In My Business."

Sylvia Rhone has dubbed Missy a genius because of her business savvy. "Missy continues to amaze me," says Rhone. "She demonstrates a great sense of adventure, a willingness to take risks. . . . She continues to give hip hop a change of face and in doing so she keeps altering the landscape of popular music."

At the same time Missy was also writing hits for established mega-stars like Whitney Houston and Destiny's Child. "It was a dream come true to get a call from Mariah [Carey], to get a call from Whitney [Houston]," she told *Interview* magazine in 1999. "Those are major people I've always dreamed of working with." She also recalled the thrill of hearing from the musicians she had idolized as a child. "So when I got a call from Janet [Jackson], just to hear her say she loved my music, it was like a blessing," she reported.

Missy's unique, conversational, light-hearted style of blending singing, rapping, and writing was completely different from anything else at the time. Missy blended her old school influences with modern beats and catchy hooks, courtesy of Timbaland, and came up with a flavor all her own. She blurred the lines between different musical genres of rock, rap, electronic music, and R&B, which lent to her massive appeal.

Missy wasn't afraid to break the rules when it came to her music. And she wasn't bothered that she didn't fit the entertainment industry's standard that female stars not be overweight. Missy was proud of her body and believed she represented other heavy women in the world. It was part of what made Missy Elliott distinctive, she told *Rolling Stone* magazine:

> **"I'm cutting edge, so I don't mind taking a chance and doing something different. Besides, I most definitely feel like you don't have to be 5'6" and a size 2 or that you got to be light-skinned with long hair to be beautiful. I feel my personality is beautiful, so that should make up for the outside."**

Success had come fast to Misdemeanor. Her debut album had gone platinum. She'd had several *Billboard* chart hits, was producing and writing for other artists, and had won over millions of new fans.

Missy Elliott performs at KKBT's Summer Jam in Irvine, California, in 1999. That same year she began work on her second album, *Da Real World*. She wanted the album to be significantly different from her first release.

4

Keeping It Fresh

Because **biter** artists were imitating *Supa Dupa Fly*, Missy decided her next album, *Da Real World*, would experiment with a whole new set of sounds. "I wanted it to be a lot different from the first album," she told Yahoo! Music in June 1999. "Since a lot of people were beat bitin', I wanted the beats on this one different."

Working with Timbaland again, Missy created the album's first hit single, "She's a Bitch." Missy explained to *Interview* magazine that the song refers to how women are often treated in the business world. At meetings she often experienced **bias** whenever she tried to voice her opinions, she explained. "When a guy expresses his feelings when he's mad, it's called aggressive," she commented, "but when a female expresses her feelings and has an attitude about stuff, she's called a bitch, and I got that from just being in meetings at my record label."

Da Real World, although not as critically acclaimed as Missy's first album, received some good reviews. However, some reviewers weren't as kind to Timbaland. He was criticized for creating similar sounds in several albums he'd worked on. In a 1999 Yahoo! Music article, Missy was quick to come to her friend's defense. "All the people Timbaland produces—me, Ginuwine, Aaliyah, himself—we all have our own different identity," she explained. "Tim knows not to give us the same thing." However, she does admit that similarities can sometimes occur: "This is one producer. It's impossible for one person to do three whole albums without using the same sound somewhere along the line."

Despite the criticism, *Da Real World* was nominated for a Grammy in 2000 for Best Rap Album. Its biggest single, "Hot Boyz," went platinum and reached number one on both the *Billboard* Rap Singles and on the R&B Singles chart. The video for "Hot Boyz" was also recognized with a Soul Train Lady of Soul Award for Best R&B/Soul or Rap video.

Battling with Herself

After producing two successful albums, Missy decided it was time for some self evaluation. She was determined to clean up her language, and to stop abusing alcohol and marijuana. Some habits were hard to break, she told *Spin* Magazine in June 1999. "I go through battles where I'm like 'Dag, I'm still cussing on albums,' and I don't wanna cuss no more. . . . I'm trying to get it together. I stopped a lot of things. . . . I won't [get] drunk and I don't smoke. . . . but I don't want people to be like 'Okay, now she's Reverend Elliott.'"

Missy also realized that as a celebrity she had to answer to public criticism. Some people had been quick to condemn her song "Busa Rhyme," from *Da Real World* album. It contained a spot by then unknown rapper Eminem, whose lyrics about punching and smacking women appeared to encourage domestic abuse. This kind of message directly contradicted the intent of Missy's latest business endeavor, a lipstick line created by IMAN Cosmetics.

Missy was donating the profits from IMAN's Misdemeanor lipstick sales to Break the Cycle, a charity organization that provides counseling and support to young people in abusive relationships. Because children who grow up with abuse are more likely to abusive in adult relationships, the group counsels young people to "break the cycle" of violence in their lives. Missy strongly believed in the program. In the hopes of reaching out and changing some of her fans' lives, she even came forward publicly and told of her own abuse. Sales of *Da Real*

Using one of her nicknames, Misdemeanor, Missy created a lipstick with IMAN Cosmetics. Some of the proceeds from the peach-colored lipstick go to support the charity Break the Cycle, which helps stop the cycle of domestic violence.

World didn't suffer much because of the Eminem controversy, but Missy had to publicly justify his appearance on her album.

A Big New Year

In May 2001 Missy released her third solo record, entitled *Miss E . . . So Addictive.* Once again Missy brought in Timbaland and also added some new guest artists, including Jay-Z, Method Man, Ludacris, Eve, Nelly Furtado, and Ginuwine. When asked by VH1 how her new album differed from *Da Real World*, Missy replied, "This album is very bright and colorful—it makes you dance; the last album was pretty dark. I think that last album was real tense 'cause I had a point to prove." With *Miss E*, Missy explained, "I was relaxed and we had mad fun in the studio."

The album's first single, "Get Ur Freak On," was described by *Rolling Stone* as "the weirdest, loudest, funkiest and just plain best single of the summer so far, a sonic orgasmatron of Indian tablas and Dirty South future-shock funk." Another solid success, it went to number one on the *Billboard* R&B/Hip-hop Airplay chart.

The "Get Ur Freak On" video, which was directed by David Meyers, proved to be Missy's oddest concoction yet, featuring a grimy, underground jungle setting and computer-enhanced creative ideas. Its innovation would be recognized with a Soul Train Lady of Soul Award for Best R&B/Soul or Rap Music Video. The video also earned six MTV Video Music Award nominations.

"Get Ur Freak On" also won Missy her first Grammy award, for Best Rap Solo Performance. The single remained at the top of the *Billboard* R&B charts for almost two months, making Missy the highest-ranking female rapper on the charts for 2001.

In September 2001 Missy's second single from *Miss E . . . So Addictive*, entitled "One Minute Man," hit the top of the charts. The song's video, again directed by Dave Meyers, featured Missy dancing in and out of hotel rooms. Through the magic of special effects, at one point Missy takes her head off and starts dancing with it. The song itself earned a Grammy nomination and its video a Soul Train Lady of Soul Award for Best R&B/Soul or Rap Music Video.

In addition to working hard on her music, 30-year-old Missy was also working on improving her health. In late 2001 she was diagnosed with hypertension, which can lead to strokes and heart attacks. After her mother suffered a serious heart attack, Missy became concerned

Missy Elliott holds up two awards at the 2002 Grammy ceremony. In addition to the award for her song "Get Ur Freak On," a song she produced, "Lady Marmalade," won a Grammy for Best Pop Collaboration.

Missy Elliott and Dave Meyers pose at a party before the MTV Video Music Awards in 2003. Dave Meyers directed many of Elliott's most outrageous and inventive videos, and together they won an MTV Video Music award for "Work It."

about her own health. She decided to lose weight by following her personal physician's recommendations to eat a more healthy diet and work out regularly.

Coping with Tragedy

At the same time Missy was trying to deal with the emotional shock of several tragedies. In August 2001 she had been devastated by the death of her friend Aaliyah, who was killed in a plane crash in the Bahamas.

Missy Elliott performs at the Step Up Women's Network and *Vanity Fair* tribute concert to Aaliyah, October 2002. Missy had contributed to Aaliyah's self-titled third album, which sold more than 6 million copies worldwide after the R&B singers death in an airplane crash.

A month later, the deadly terrorist attacks of September 11 killed several thousand people at New York City's World Trade Center and shocked the nation. As Missy struggled to come to terms with these deaths, she began working on her next album, which she called *Under Construction*. It would reflect a more serious tone, addressing the fragility of life. The sudden death of yet another good friend and fellow artist, Lisa "Left Eye" Lopes, in April 2002 kept Missy focused on the messages she wanted her album to contain.

For Missy, the year 2002 became a time of rebuilding and remembering those who had passed on. During that year, she brought about changes in her physical self, eventually dropping 70 pounds from her weight. And she came to terms with her emotional self, as she created songs that expressed her feelings of sorrow and loss, particularly with Aaliyah's death.

In *Under Construction*, which was released in November 2002, Missy uses the opening interlude on the album to discuss her new-found perspective on life. In the track she also calls for peace between feuding rappers, and requests that life be celebrated and not wasted over trivial matters. Old friend Timbaland helped Missy once again by providing the beats for the album and appearing in a guest spot. The album also features appearances by Jay-Z, Ludacris, Beyoncé Knowles, TLC, and Method Man.

Working with Dave Meyers again on the video for the album's first single, "Work It," Missy set out to share her imagination. "I try to keep my videos as unique as possible," she told MTV News in October 2002. "I know that when I'm in the studio rhyming, I'm visually thinking about it and that is what I want people to see."

The video features Missy dancing—sometimes suspended in midair—in an abandoned playground, subway station, and an old dance club, among other settings. The break dancing routine and the old school Adidas jumpsuits worn by Missy and the dancers illustrate her desire to bring hip-hop back to its roots. In a few shots, Missy pays tribute to Aaliyah and Left Eye: their faces are painted on the hood of a car above the words "In Loving Memory."

"Work It" was an enormous hit. After the single's release in November 2002, it remained at the top of both the *Billboard* R&B/Hip-hop Singles & Tracks Chart and the R&B Hip-hop Airplay Chart for five weeks. In 2003 the song won Missy an American Music Award and another Grammy, as well as several nominations in other categories. The

This picture of Missy Elliott, depicting her performance of "Get Ur Freak On" at the 2001 MTV Video Music Awards, was part of a display put up by the music channel in New York's Rockefeller Center. The pieces showed famous moments in music video history.

song's video proved just as successful, garnering several awards, including a Soul Train Lady of Soul Award and two MTV Video Music Awards.

By July 2003 *Under Construction* was certified double platinum, becoming Missy's most commercially successful album. It featured several other successful singles, including "Gossip Folks," "Knoc" (featuring Knoc-Turn'Al and Dr. Dre), "Burning Up" (featuring Faith Evans), "Scream aka Itchin," and "Crew Deep" (with Skillz and Kandi).

Missy Elliott made her film debut in 2003, with a cameo role in the 2003 movie *Honey*. In the film Missy shows up to watch a performance at a dance studio. She is pictured in this scene arguing with a video director.

A Collaboration Machine

In the fall of 2003 Missy and other musical performers, including Eve, Tweet, and Aimee Mann, performed in the "Where My Girls At" tour. Missy had organized the three concerts, held in New York, Chicago, and Los Angeles, as a tribute to Aaliyah. Its proceeds went to Break the Cycle, for which Missy now served as official spokesperson.

Although Missy was busy planning shows and winning awards in 2003, she still had time to do what she loved best: writing and collaborating on others' records. She did a guest spot on Timbaland and Magoo's "Cop That Disc" single. She also made a cameo appearance playing herself in the movie *Honey*, directed by Bille Woodruff, and guested with Beyoncé Knowles, MC Lyte, and Free on the soundtrack to the movie *The Fighting Temptations*. And she also found the time to record yet another album.

Missy Elliott holds her award from the First Annual Vibe Awards, November 2003. The Vibe Awards were created to honor innovation and creativity in urban music. Missy won in the "Reelest Video" category for her video "Work It."

5

Queen of
the Hill

When Missy released her fourth album, *This Is Not a Test*, in November 2003, she was an established superstar. However, she continued seeking ways to change and improve herself and her work. Toward the end of 2003 she decided that the nickname Misdemeanor no longer represented who she was. From that point on, she would be simply Missy Elliott.

Missy was feeling positive when she released *This Is Not a Test*. She told MTV that "this album represents how I feel right now in my life. I'm in good space, and I think you can hear that." Although the songs were in typical Missy style, she made a major change in that Timbaland did not produce all of the album's beat tracks. This time around, new contributors like Craig Brockman, the Soul Diggaz, and Nisan Stewart lent their talents to the record.

On the album Missy was bolder than ever with the sexual lyrics in some songs. In others, such as "Wake Up," in which fellow rapper Jay-Z guests, Missy again touched on the message she shared in *Under Construction*: life is fragile—don't waste it by focusing on material belongings and being petty. Other guest stars included the Clark Sisters, Mary J. Blige, and Elephant Man.

The record also included more of Missy's trademark party music, featuring unique beats done by Timbaland. *This Is Not a Test*'s first single, "Pass That Dutch" was another throwback to the old school rap Missy loved so much. The song's title alludes to a hit called "Pass the Dutchie," by the 1980s reggae band Musical Youth.

The "Pass That Dutch" video, produced by Dave Meyers, stirred up quite a bit of controversy with Missy's fans. She had previously appeared in videos wearing large baggy jogging suits and loose clothing, but this time around a much slimmer Missy sported short skirts and tight-fitting outfits. Dismayed fans believed Missy's weight loss showed that she had caved in to pressure from the music industry. To make matters worse, one segment of the video featured Missy riding in a jeep with four heavy-set ladies while rapping, "If you's a fat one, put your clothes back on/Before you start putting potholes in my lawn."

Missy received so much negative feedback that she posted a response to her outraged fans on her Web site. In her message, she explained her reasons for losing weight, citing her hypertension and her mother's heart attack. "I was very disturbed to find that a few people were angry at my weight loss," Missy wrote. "To all my fans who are upset about this, I still represent for overweight adults and kids but I am also now painfully and personally aware of the health issues." She also apologized for any offense caused by her lines in the "Pass That Dutch" video:

> **"I simply meant that you should dress right for your body size. I have always been a big girl myself and I always took pride in the fact that I never had to change my body to be considered beautiful or success-ful. I think I have always represented [that you should have] pride in yourself no matter what size you are."**

Missy concluded the Web site message by asking her fans to support her in her effort to stay healthy.

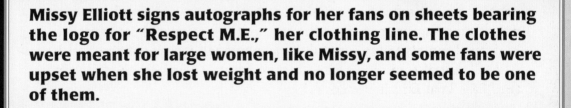

Missy Elliott signs autographs for her fans on sheets bearing the logo for "Respect M.E.," her clothing line. The clothes were meant for large women, like Missy, and some fans were upset when she lost weight and no longer seemed to be one of them.

Such a Busy Woman

By March of 2004 Missy was ready to go out on the road. This time she shared the stage with Beyoncé Knowles and Alicia Keys. Their Ladies First Tour, also known as The Triple Threat, became one of the highest grossing events for 2004, raking in around $19 million in one month.

Missy brought UPN network cameras along during the tour to film a reality show she'd been planning. Broadcast the following year as *The Road to Stardom with Missy Elliott,* the show featured 13 singers, rappers, and dancers competing against one another for a $100,000 recording contract with Missy's label.

In addition to making music, Missy was also accepting offers to make commercials and endorse products such as Sprite and Gap jeans. In 2003 she appeared with pop star Madonna in a television commercial for Gap. And in 2004, M.A.C cosmetics selected her as a spokesperson for its Viva Glam campaign.

That same year Missy signed a deal with Adidas to create a line of women's athletic apparel. The sneakers, tracksuits, hooded sweatshirts, and t-shirts feature a logo designed by Missy that includes the words "Respect M.E.," (a motto that uses her initials but also makes a statement about respecting the person wearing the clothing). The Respect M.E. apparel is designed to fit women of all sizes, and a portion of the sales is donated to Missy's favorite charity, Break the Cycle.

Meanwhile Missy's contributions to the music industry continued to receive acclaim. In June the cable network Black Entertainment Television gave her the BET Award for Female Hip-hop Artist of the year. She also received nominations for two MTV Video Music Awards for a second video from *This Is Not a Test,* for the single "I'm Really Hot."

In August, while the country was getting ready for the 2004 presidential elections, Missy was hard at work on a single to encourage young people to vote on Election Day. Entitled "Wake Up Everybody," the song featured a collaboration of hip-hop and R&B artists including Mary J. Blige, Monica, Eve, Brandy, Fabolous, Ashanti, Jadakiss, Wyclef Jean, MC Lyte, and Jamie Foxx, as well as Missy.

An entirely different kind of music single, by Missy and Christina Aguilera, hit the top 40 that September. The two had collaborated on a remake of the 1976 song "Car Wash," which was featured in the animated film *Shark Tale.* That same month Ghostface Killah's song "Push," in which Missy helped with remixes, went to number one on the Billboard Hot Dance Music Club Play chart.

Missy continued to display her golden touch on several more collaborations. She was featured with R&B vocalist Ciara on her song "1, 2 Step" on her debut album *Goodies.* In February 2005 the single reached the top of the Billboard Hot Dance Radio Airplay chart and

Madonna and Missy Elliott shoot a commercial for Gap's 2003 fall campaign—an indication of the mainstream success Missy had achieved. Like Madonna, Missy is a strong woman who is not afraid to show an attitude. This makes her popular among female audiences.

**Some of the collaborators on the animated film *Shark Tale*—
Mary J. Blige, Renée Zellweger, Angelina Jolie, Missy Elliott,
and Christina Aguilera—attend the movie's premiere in
September 2004. Missy Elliott provided the song "Car Wash"
for the soundtrack.**

remained there for two weeks. Missy also collaborated with *American
Idol* winner Fantasia Barrino on her debut album, *Free Yourself*, in
November 2004. Yet another Grammy nomination, this time for Best
Rap Song, came Missy's way for her work on the disc.

Does Missy Ever Sleep?

Somewhere in between collaborating and writing, Missy found time
to work on her own music. In June 2005 she released her first self-
produced single, entitled "Lose Control," which featured Ciara and
Fatman Scoop. The song became a Top-40 hit and eventually reached
the Top 10. It was included on Missy's sixth album, *The Cookbook*,
which hit the stores in July.

In *The Cookbook* Missy decided that the majority of songs would
be done by several new producers, although Timbaland offered his

advice and produced two tracks on the album. Kwame, Scott Storch, Rich Harrison, and Pharrell of the Neptunes produced the rest. The album featured guest spots by Slick Rick, Mary J. Blige, Tweet, and Mike Jones, among others.

However, Missy didn't stray from her usual formula for the making of *The Cookbook* music videos. The "Lose Control" video, which featured kung fu fight scenes and dancers suspended in midair,

Missy Elliott accepts her MTV Video Music Award for Best Dance Video in 2005. She won for the video for "Lose Control" from her album *The Cookbook*. She also won a VMA for "Lose Control" for Best Hip-Hop Video.

was directed as usual by Dave Meyers. It received nominations for five MTV Video Music Awards, and won two of them in August 2005. The following year, the video would also earn Missy yet another Grammy, this time for Best Short Form Music Video.

Off Her Feet—For a Minute

In September 2005 Missy suffered an injury that threatened to slow her down. While practicing a dance routine, she tore her Achilles tendon and required surgery to repair the tear. Because her recovery would take several months, she had to cancel some appearances. However, although she couldn't dance, she still managed to keep her schedule full.

In November 2005, with the aid of a wheelchair and crutches, Missy attended the American Music Awards, where she was honored as the Favorite Female Artist: Rap/Hip-Hop. At the ceremony Missy mentioned that she had been writing an autobiographical screenplay. Plans for bringing Missy's story to the big screen were under way in the spring of 2006. Director Dianne Houston explained the basis of the film to *NowPlaying* magazine:

> **"What's compelling about [the story] is that Missy is a survivor. . . . as a child; [she] had to create other realities in order to survive what she was going through. In a lesser person, she would have become a victim or bitter, but instead it fueled this creative spark and this amazing art in her."**

That December Missy's art could be heard on the single "Ultimate Rush" in the posthumous release album *Duets: The Final Chapter* for Notorious B.I.G. She also lent a hand to Ashlee Simpson's single "L.O.V.E. (The Missy Underground Mix)." And she continued to work with Adidas to design only the freshest apparel for her Respect M.E. line of clothing.

Fully mended by January 2006, Missy began filming her video for "We Run This" with Dave Meyers. The single also serves as the theme song for the 2006 film *Stick It*, which Missy helped score. The video follows the gymnastics theme of the movie: Missy, while being coached by Olympic gold-medalist Dominique Dawes, performs a balance beam routine on skyscraper girders and swings on a set of uneven bars in a basement laundry room.

Despite a leg injury, Missy Elliot performs during an October 2005 concert while riding a motor scooter. She was still recovering from an injury to her Achilles' tendon at the time, but did not want to take more time off.

Surrounded by her fans and admirers, Missy Elliott hosts MTV's *Total Request Live* in April 2006. Since its debut in 1998, *TRL* has become MTV's flagship show, and is the only program on the channel that still routinely airs music videos.

A Music Icon

Missy Elliott is one of the hardest working and most talented females in hip-hop today. She has sold more than 12 million of her own albums and contributed to the success of many other artists. Yet, she remains modest about her accomplishments. When honored at the 2005 American Music Awards, where she was referred to as a hip-hop icon, she accepted the award with humility. "I ain't no icon," she commented later. "I'm just Missy, I'm just crazy, that's all."

Where will the future lead Missy Elliott? It is hard to imagine what she will come up with next. Her creative mind is always at work, and incredible new ideas are always blossoming. If she maintains her current pace, Missy will be raising the bar for artists for many years to come.

1971 Melissa "Missy" Arnette Elliott is born on July 1 in Portsmouth, Virginia.

1984 Missy's mother, Patricia Elliott, separates from her husband, Ronnie Elliott, and takes custody of their daughter.

1991 Missy forms an R&B group called Fay-Z and begins writing songs with Tim "Timbaland" Mosely. Fay-Z is signed to Elektra as Sista.

1994 Sista's record is dropped from the Elektra label.

1995 Missy joins DeVante Swing's writing and production team. She writes and produces multiple hits for SWV, 702, and other groups.

1996 Missy and Timbaland write and produce songs for Aaliyah's album *One in a Million*, which goes double platinum. Missy begins to use the nickname Misdemeanor.

1997 Elektra CEO Sylvia Rhone signs Missy to Elektra. She creates her own label, The Gold Mind, Inc., and releases her first solo album, *Supa Dupa Fly*. Her first video, for "The Rain (Supa Dupa Fly)," is nominated for three MTV Video Music Awards and wins two Billboard Music Awards.

1998 Missy receives nominations for three Grammy Awards.

1999 In June Missy releases her second album, *Da Real World*, and its single "Hot Boyz" goes platinum. Missy becomes involved with the charity organization Break the Cycle; she designates a portion of the proceeds from Misdemeanor lipstick, produced by IMAN Cosmetics, to go the organization.

2000 Missy is nominated for a Grammy for Best Rap Album and wins a Soul Train Lady of Soul award.

2001 Missy is honored that March with a Heroes Award by the National Academy of Recording Arts and Sciences (NARAS) for her work with Break the Cycle and her participation in NARAS's Grammy in the Schools program. In May she releases her third album, *Miss E . . . So Addictive*. In August Missy's friend and fellow artist Aaliyah is killed in a plane crash.

2002 In February Missy receives a Grammy Award for Best Rap Solo Performance ("Get Ur Freak On"). In November she releases her third album, *Under Construction*.

2003 In February Missy wins a Grammy for 2002 Best Female Rap Solo Performance. *Under Construction* goes double platinum in July. That November, the American Music Awards honors her as a favorite rap/hip-hop female artist, and she releases her fourth album, *This Is Not A Test*. Missy decides to drop the nickname Misdemeanor.

2004 Missy wins a Grammy for 2003 Best Female Rap Solo Performance. Beyoncé Knowles and Alicia Keys join her in the Ladies First Tour. She begins filming a reality TV show, *The Road to Stardom with Missy Elliott*, and helps to create the Respect M.E. Adidas clothing line.

2005 In July Missy releases her fifth album, *The Cookbook*, and its single "Lose Control," goes triple platinum. The American Music Awards again honor her as favorite hip-hop female artist.

2006 Missy collaborates with Mike Simpson of the Dust Brothers to score film *Stick It*, which features "We Run This" as its theme song. In February she takes home a fourth Grammy, for 2005 Best Short Form Music Video.

Albums

1997 *Supa Dupa Fly*

1999 *Da Real World*

2001 *Miss E . . . So Addictive*

2002 *Under Construction*

2003 *This Is Not a Test*

2005 *The Cookbook*

Major Music Awards

1997 Winner, *Billboard* Video Music Awards for Best Clip (Rap) and Best New Artist Clip (Rap) for "The Rain (Supa Dupa Fly)"

1999 *The Rain (Supa Dupa Fly)* is included in *MTV: 100 Greatest Videos Ever Made*

2000 Winner, Soul Train Lady of Soul Award for Best R&B/Soul or Rap Music Video, for "Hot Boyz"

2001 Winner, Soul Train Lady of Soul Award for Best R&B/Soul or Rap Music Video, for "Get Ur Freak On"

2002 Winner, Grammy Award for Best Rap Solo Performance, for "Get Ur Freak On"

Winner, Soul Train Lady of Soul Award for Best R&B/Soul or Rap Music Video, for "Get Ur Freak On"

Winner, BET Award for Best Female Hip-hop Artist, for "One Minute Man"

2003 Winner, Grammy Award for Best Solo Rap Performance— Female, for "Scream aka Itchin"

Winner, Soul Train Lady of Soul Award for Best R&B/Soul or Rap Music Video, for "Work It"

Winner, BET Award for Best Female Hip-hop Artist

Winner of two Soul Train Lady of Soul Awards: Best Song and Best Music Video, for "Work It"

Winner of two MTV Video Music Awards: Video of the Year and Best Hip-hop Video

Winner, American Music Award for Favorite Rap/Hip-hop Female Artist

2004   Winner, Grammy Award for Best Rap Solo Performance— Female, for "Work It"

Winner, BET Award for Female Hip-hop Artist of the Year

2005   Winner of two MTV Video Music Awards: Best Dance Video and Best Hip-hop Video, for "Lose Control"

Winner, American Music Award for Favorite Rap/Hip-hop Female Artist

Winner, Grammy Award for Best Music Video, Short Form, for "Lose Control"

Books

Ehrlich, Dimitri. "Music's Anti-Hero, Anti-Cliché, Anti-Formula Pro." *Interview*, May 2001.

Morgan, Joan. "The Making of Miss Thang! Rap Singer Missy Elliott." *Essence*, March 2000.

Musto, Michael. "Master Missy—Writer, Singer, Producer and Label Head Missy Elliott." *Interview*, June 1999.

"Rhymes and Misdemeanor." *Rolling Stone*. August 6, 1997.

Sheffield, Rob. "Missy Elliott: Miss E . . . So Addictive." *Rolling Stone*. June 21, 2001.

Simon, Brent. "Latest Rap Act to Go Big Screen: Missy Elliott." *NowPlaying.* March 30, 2006.

VIBE Books. *Hip-hop Diva*, New York: Three Rivers Press. 2001.

Vineyard, Jennifer. "Missy Elliott Re-Launches Gold Mind Label." *Rolling Stone*, June 7, 2000.

Web Sites

www.Missy-Elliott.com
Missy Elliott's official website, featuring her biography, music, tour dates, and additional information.

www.rollingstone.com/MissyElliott
Rolling Stone magazine's online collection includes articles, interviews, and reviews with information about Missy and her work.

www.VH1.com/artists/az/elliott_missy/artist.jhtml
VH1's online collection of articles, interviews, reviews, multimedia and more about Missy.

www.breakthecycle.org
The Web Site for Break the Cycle, an organization that works to engage, educate, and empower youth to build lives and communities free of domestic violence. Missy serves as official spokesperson for Break the Cycle and helps provide financial support.

www.AtlanticRecords.com
In 2004 Elektra merged with Atlantic Records, which runs Missy's label The Gold Mind, Inc. This Web site provides a link to the latest news about her albums and other work.

audition—a trial performance by an actor, dancer, or musician, to demonstrate suitability or skill.

bias—a personal and often unreasoned judgment for or against one side in a dispute.

biter—an artist who copies others' styles and claims them as his or her own.

collaborate—to work together toward a common goal.

contemporary—current and/or modern.

double platinum—an award granted by the Recording Industry Association of America signifying 2 million records sold.

genre—a type, class, or category, usually referring to music.

Grammy—music award given by the National Academy of Recording Arts and Sciences for excellence in the recording industry.

Misdemeanor—a crime that carries a less severe punishment than a felony; Missy Elliott's early nickname.

old school hip-hop—early hip-hop music of the 1970s and early 1980s

platinum—an award granted by the Recording Industry Association of America signifying 1 million records sold.

remix—new version of a song, usually upbeat so it is easy to dance to, made using techniques of audio editing.

sampling—taking an actual piece of another artist's music and using it in a new song.

solace—a source of comfort.

Michelle Lawlor is a freelance writer and photographer with a keen interest in music journalism. A resident of central New Jersey, she spends her free time listening to music and taking photographs of local music ensembles. This is her first biography.

Picture Credits

page

2: KRT/James Keivom
8: Everrett Collection
11: Michelle Feng/NMI
12: Michelle Feng/NMI
14: PRNewsFoto/NMI
17: Zuma Press/CLS/F.KOK
19: Michelle Feng/NMI
20: Zuma Press/Bandphoto/UPPA
22: Zuma Press/CLS/F.KOK
25: Big Pictures USA
27: Walter Weissman/Star Max
29: Michelle Feng/NMI
30: Zuma Press/Nancy Kaszerman
32: Zuma Press/Vaughn Youtz

35: KRT/NMI
37: KRT/Nicholas Khayat
38: Ronald Asadorian/Splash News
39: Zuma Press/Fernando Salas
41: Brian Prahl/Splash News
42: Zuma Press/Universal Studios
44: Zuma Press/Janice Yim
47: Mario Anzuoni/Splash News
49: PRNewsFoto/NMI
50: Features Photo Services/NMI
51: Zuma Press/NMI
53: Zuma Press/Aviv Small
54: Michael Loccisano/FilmMagic

Front cover: SHNS/Elektra Entertainment Group
Back cover: UPI/Laura Cavanaugh